What's this? *It's a (bike).*	*What colour is it?* *It's (green).*	*What day is it tod* *It's (Thursday).*

Phonics	Culture	Literacy	Cross-curricular links
Consonant sound **r**: **r**ed **r**abbit **r**ed **r**uler	School assembly	A classroom poster	**Science:** Tidy classroom; School subjects; Lining up **Arts and Crafts:** Lines and shapes
Consonant sound **s**: **s**ix **s**nakes **s**low **s**cooter	Birthday parties	A birthday card	**Science:** The senses **Arts and Crafts:** Patterns
Consonant sound **h**: **H**elen **h**appy **h**ippo **h**ops **h**ops	Circus Day	An action rhyme	**Science:** Similarities and differences; What the body can do; Emotions and feelings **Arts and Crafts:** Lines and colours
This is my (father / mother). *His / Her name is ...*		Making a class Christmas tree	**Science:** Different types of family **Arts and Crafts:** Art in my home
Consonant sound **j**: **J**im **j**uggles **j**am **j**uice **j**elly	A traditional English breakfast	A lunch menu	**Science:** Hot and cold food; Healthy food; Vegetables; Meals of the day **Arts and Crafts:** Texture
Consonant sound **sh**: **sh**ush! **sh**out **sh**eep	Urban farms	Animal riddles	**Science:** Farm animals and domestic animals; How animals move; Wild animals **Arts and Crafts:** Forms
Consonant sound **w**: **W**ally **w**orm **w**ashes **w**indows	Parks	A seed packet	**Science:** Living and non-living things; What plants need to survive **Arts and Crafts:** Geometric and natural shapes
What's the weather like today? *It's (windy).*		Making a class spring wall display	**Science:** Clothing in different weather **Arts and Crafts:** Art in My World
Consonant sound **z**: la**z**y **z**ebra **z**oo	Cycling	A fable	**Science:** Safety rules in the street; Transport **Arts and Crafts:** Buildings and symmetry
Consonant sound **v**: **V**icky **v**et lo**v**es **v**olleyball	Camping in the garden	A postcard	**Science:** Human and physical elements in the environment **Arts and Crafts:** Landscapes
Consonant sound **th**: **th**ree **th**in ba**th** **Th**ursday	The Tooth Fairy	A poem	**Science:** Daytime and nighttime activities; Daytime and nighttime sky and animals **Arts and Crafts:** Warm and cool colours
He's / She's wearing (a blue T-shirt). *There's (a torch) in his / her rucksack.*		Making a group holiday poster	**Science:** Materials **Arts and Crafts:** Recycled Art

Starter Unit

Lesson 1

Hello, friends!

1 Listen and point. Sing *What's your name?* CD1 2

2 Say *The ten balloons* chant. CD1 4

3 Find, count and write.

10  balloons

 bananas

 balls

 hats

 socks

 books

 dogs

 bike

Vocabulary: numbers 1-10
Grammar: *Hello. Goodbye. What's your name? I'm (Jake).*

High Five! ENGLISH

PUPIL'S BOOK 1

S	Hello, friends!	page 4
1	Ready for school!	page 8
2	Happy birthday!	page 18
3	At the circus	page 28
	My project 1: Family	page 38
4	Fantastic food!	page 42
5	Fun on the farm	page 52
6	A day in the park	page 62
	My project 2: Spring	page 72
7	Let's explore my town!	page 76
8	Camping fun!	page 86
9	Day and night	page 96
	My project 3: Holidays	page 106
	Festivals: Christmas	page 110
	Festivals: Easter	page 111

My name is ______________________________.

MACMILLAN

Donna Shaw • Joanne Ramsden

Course consultants: Rocío Gutiérrez Burgos and Mónica Pérez Is

Contents

S Hello, friends!	Numbers 1-10 Shapes Colours Days of the week	*Hello.* *Goodbye.* *What's your name?* *I'm (Jake).*
	Vocabulary	**Grammar**
1 Ready for school!	Classroom objects More classroom objects	*Where's my (pencil)? It's here.* *Put the (book) on the (shelf).* *in / on / under*
2 Happy birthday!	Toys Adjectives	*What is it?* *Is it a (bike)?* *Yes, it is. No, it isn't.* *What's your favourite toy* *My favourite toy is a (ba*
3 At the circus	Parts of the body Describing hair and eyes	*I've got a (red nose).* *I've got (small eyes).* *My friend has got (long hair).* *He's / She's got (blue eyes).*
My project 1: Family	Family members	*Have you got (a brother)?* *Yes, I have. No, I haven't.*
4 Fantastic food!	Food Fruit	*I like (chicken).* *I love (ice cream).* *I don't like (fish).* *Do you like (grapes)?* *Yes, I do. No, I don't.*
5 Fun on the farm	Farm animals Actions	*Can you see a (cow)?* *Yes, I can. No, I can't.* *(Birds) can fly. (Pigs) can't climb.*
6 A day in the park	Playground objects and nature Prepositions	*Where's (Beth)?* *He's / She's (on the swing).* *Where are (Jake and Molly)?* *They're (behind) the (tree).*
My project 2: Spring	Spring animals and plants Weather	*How many (flowers) can you see?* *I can see (seven) flowers.*
7 Let's explore my town!	Places in the town Transport Numbers 11-20	*There's a (zoo).* *There are (two sweet shops).* *How many (cars) are there?*
8 Camping fun!	Clothes Outdoor activities	*What are you wearing?* *I'm wearing (shorts) and a (T-shirt).* *What's he / she doing?* *He's / She's (riding a horse).*
9 Day and night	Daily routines Meal times	*I (wash my face) every day.* *I have (dinner in the evening).*
My project 3: Holidays	Places for a holiday Holiday things	*What's your favourite place?* *My favourite place is (the mountains).*
Festivals	Christmas	Easter

1 Listen and repeat. Act out. CD1 5

2 Listen and find. Point. CD1 6

3 Point. Ask and answer.

What's this? It's a balloon.

4 Find these shapes in the picture.

circle rectangle square triangle oval

Vocabulary: shapes
Grammar: *What's this? It's a (bike).*

1 Listen and read. Act out. CD1 7

A big surprise

Vocabulary: colours
Grammar: *What colour is it? It's green.*

1 Listen and sing *Seven days a week*.

CD1 8

Monday, Tuesday,
Wednesday, Thursday,
Friday, Saturday and Sunday.

Seven days a week.
Seven days a week.
We ride our magic bike,
Seven days a week.

2 Listen. Ask and answer.

CD1 9 Talk Partners

Vocabulary: days of the week
Grammar: *What day is it today? It's (Thursday).*

Ready for school!

1 Listen and point. Sing *I'm ready for school!*

CD1 11

A pen, a pencil,
A crayon, too.
I'm ready! I'm ready!
I'm ready for school!

A rubber, a ruler,
A sharpener, too.
I'm ready! I'm ready!
I'm ready for school!

A book, a school bag,
A pencil case, too.
I'm ready! I'm ready!
I'm ready for school!
Hurray! I'm ready for school!

2 Read and stick the ten stickers. Listen and say the chant.

CD1 13

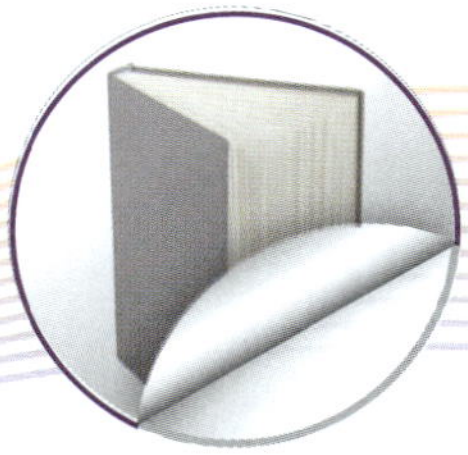

book | pen | rubber | pencil | ruler

Vocabulary: classroom objects

Learning to LEARN **Spelling:** Activity Book page 15

1 Listen and repeat. Act out. CD1 14

Grammar
Where's my pencil?
It's here.

2 Listen and find. Circle. CD1 15

crayon | sharpener | computer | school bag | pencil case

Before you read What classroom objects can you see in the story?

1 Listen and read. Act out. CD1 16

Toby goes to school

Language reinforcement and input: *Where's my purple pencil case? Put the pencil case on the desk.*

High Five! values

2 Read and circle.

Keep the classroom tidy.
Put ***books / crayons / rubbish*** in the bin.

Lesson 4 Vocabulary and Grammar

1 Listen, point and say.

CD1 17

shelf

cupboard

bin

desk

board

chair

2 Listen and point. Sing *Let's tidy up*.

CD1 18

Put the book on the shelf,
On the shelf, on the shelf.
Put the book on the shelf.
Let's tidy up!

Put the paper in the bin.
In the bin, in the bin.
Put the paper in the bin.
Let's tidy up!

Put the chair under the desk,
Under the desk, under the desk.
Put the chair under the desk.
Let's tidy up!

3 Listen and repeat. Play a game.

CD1 19

Talk Partners

Vocabulary: classroom objects
Grammar: *Put the (book on the shelf). in / on / under*

TOBY'S TONGUE TWISTER

1 Listen and say. CD1 21

r – r – r. A red rabbit on a red ruler.

2 Listen and match. CD1 22

3 Make and play the game (Activity Book page 105).

British Culture

1 **Listen and read. Answer.** CD1 23

Hello! I'm Alex.

And I'm Lucy. We go to primary school in England. At school, we have an assembly every day.

1 We sit on the floor with all the children in our school. We listen to the head teacher.

2 We play music and we sing songs.

3 We clap our hands when boys and girls do good work.

Think about your culture **What do you do every day at school?**

Teacher 6-4=2 School

Literacy TEXT TYPE: A CLASSROOM POSTER

Before you read

1 Who are the good children? Circle.

2 Listen and read the classroom poster. CD1 25

Class rules

Listen to others.

Put your hand up to speak.

Work quietly.

Sit down on your chair.

Walk in the classroom.

Tidy up your things.

After you read

Go to page 12 in your Activity Book.

1 **Listen and number. Write and say.** CD1 26

computer crayon pen rubber pencil ruler
pencil case ~~sharpener~~ school bag book

1 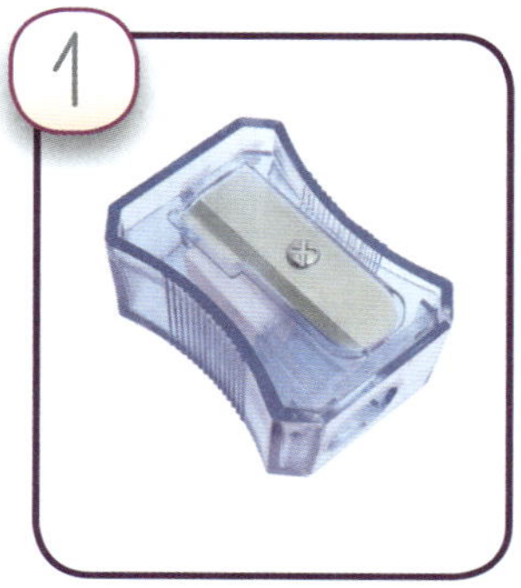

________ ________ ________ sharpener ________

________ ________ ________ ________ ________

________ ________

2 **Read and look. Write *in, on* or *under*.**

1 The school bag is under the chair.
2 The pencil case is ________ the school bag.
3 The ruler is ________ the school bag.
4 The rubber is ________ the chair.

3 **Cooperative learning:** Sing *Well done!* CD1 27

External exams practice

1 Listen and colour. There is one example. CD1 28

2 Listen. Ask and answer. CD1 29

Unit 2

Lesson 1 Vocabulary

Happy birthday!

1 Listen and point. Sing *Happy birthday!* CD1 30

Happy birthday!
Happy birthday to you!
Here's a present,
A present for you.

Is it a doll?
Is it a train?
Is it a kite
or a computer game?

Chorus

Is it a robot?
Is it a ball?
Is it a scooter
or a dinosaur?

Chorus

2 Read and stick the ten stickers. Listen and say the chant. CD1 32

ball train car doll kite

Vocabulary: toys

Learning to LEARN

Spelling: Activity Book page 25

1 Listen and repeat. Act out.

CD1 33

Grammar

What is it?
Is it a bike?
Yes, it is.
No, it isn't.

2 Listen and circle.

CD1 34

1

2

3

4

robot

scooter

teddy

dinosaur

computer game

Before you read

1 **Listen and read. Act out.** CD1 35

The slow scooter

Language reinforcement and input: *What is it? It's a motor. My scooter is slow.*

High Five! values

2 **Read and circle.**

When a person helps you, say ***hello* / *please* / *thank you*.**

1 Listen, point and say.

CD1 36

big small old new fast slow

2 Listen and point. Sing *My favourite toy*.

CD1 37

My favourite toy is a train.
My favourite toy is a train.
It's fast. It's new.
It's red and blue.
My favourite toy is a train.

My favourite toy is a teddy.
My favourite toy is a teddy.
It's old. It's big.
It's brown and pink.
My favourite toy is a teddy.

3 Listen and repeat. Ask and answer.

CD1 38

Talk Partners

Vocabulary: adjectives
Grammar: *What's your favourite toy? My favourite toy is a (ball).*

1 Listen and say. CD1 40

TOBY'S TONGUE TWISTER

2 Listen and number. CD1 41

3 **Cooperative learning:** Sing *Sharing is a good thing to do.* CD1 42

4 Make and play the game (Activity Book page 105).

British Culture

1 Listen and read. Answer.

CD1 43

It's my birthday today. I'm seven. I have a party on my birthday.

1 My party is a fancy dress party. Look! We're pirates today.

2 I've got lots of birthday cards. They're fantastic!

3 I play party games in the garden with my friends. It's good fun!

4 I've got a birthday cake with seven candles.

Think about your culture Do you have a party on your birthday?

Literacy TEXT TYPE: A BIRTHDAY CARD

Before you read

1 What can you see on the birthday card? Circle and say.

dog seven bike dinosaur scooter kite present balloons six birthday cake

2 Listen and read the birthday card. CD1 45

To Beth,

Happy Birthday

Have a fantastic party with your friends.

Lots of love,
from
Mum and Dad
x x x

After you read

Go to page 22 in your Activity Book.

1 Listen and number. Write and say. CD1 46

train kite ball scooter teddy car
robot doll computer game ~~dinosaur~~

____

____

____

____

____

____

____

____

1 
dinosaur

____

2 Look at the pictures. Read and write the toy.

1 My favourite toy is old and brown. teddy

2 My favourite toy is new and green. ____

3 My favourite toy is big and red. ____

4 My favourite toy is fast and blue. ____

3 Cooperative learning: Sing *Well done!* CD1 47

External exams practice

1 Listen and draw lines. There is one example. CD1 48

2 Listen. Ask and answer. CD1 49 Talk Partners

Unit 3

Lesson 1 Vocabulary

At the circus

1 **Listen and point. Sing *This is me*.** CD2 1

This is my body,
This is me.
This is my body.
Count with me.

Two feet,
Ten toes,
Two eyes,
One big nose.

Chorus

Ten fingers,
One head,
Two arms,
Two long legs.

2 **Read and stick the ten stickers. Listen and say the chant.** CD2 3

head legs feet toes arms

Vocabulary:
parts of the body

Learning to LEARN

Spelling: Activity Book page 35

1 Listen and repeat. Act out.

CD2 4

Grammar

I've got a red nose.
I've got big ears.

2 Listen and draw.

CD2 5

1 2 3 4

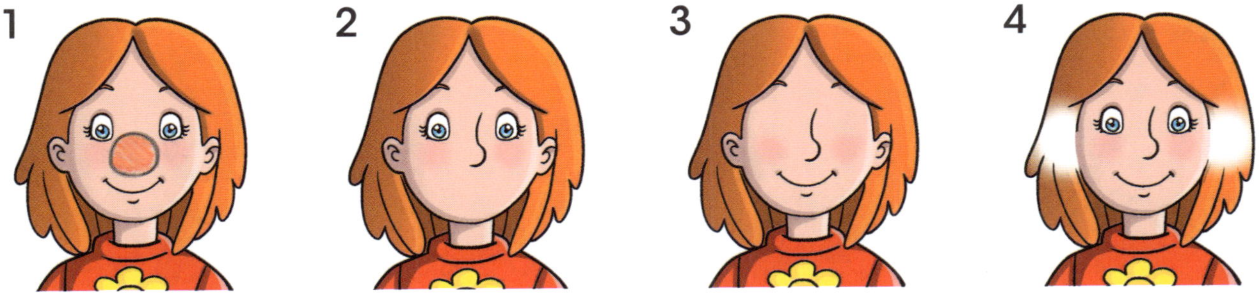

ears mouth eyes nose fingers

Before you read Can you see a clown in the story?

1 **Listen and read. Act out.** CD2 6

Fun at the circus

Language reinforcement and input:
I've got big feet. He's got purple hair.

High Five! values

2 **Read and circle.**

When you ride a bike, wear a helmet and use two ***hands*** / ***fingers*** / ***toes***.

1 Listen, point and say. CD2 7

long hair

short hair

blonde hair

brown hair

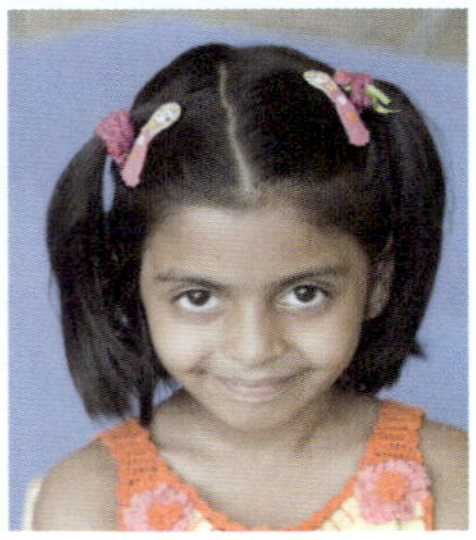

black hair

red hair

2 Listen and point. Sing *My friend*. CD2 8

I've got a friend called Jake.
He's got green eyes.
He's got short hair.
He's fantastic!

We're different
And that's OK.
We're different.
And we're friends.

I've got a friend called Beth.
She's got brown eyes.
She's got long hair.
She's fantastic!

3 Listen and repeat. Talk about your friend. CD2 9

Talk Partners

Vocabulary: describing hair and eyes
Grammar: *My friend has got (long hair). He's / She's got (blue eyes).*

1 Listen and say. CD2 11

h – h – h. Helen the happy hippo hops and hops.

2 Listen and number. CD2 12

3 Make and play the game (Activity Book page 107).

British Culture

1 Listen and read. Answer. CD2 13

'Circus Day' is a special day at our school. We paint our faces. We do different circus activities, too.

1 I spin a plate. It's very difficult. Look!

2 I juggle scarves. It's fun!

3 I ride a special bike. My teacher helps me.

4 I walk on stilts. Look! I've got long legs.

Think about your culture Do you go to the circus with your family?

Literacy TEXT TYPE: AN ACTION RHYME

Before you read

1 How are you today? Circle.

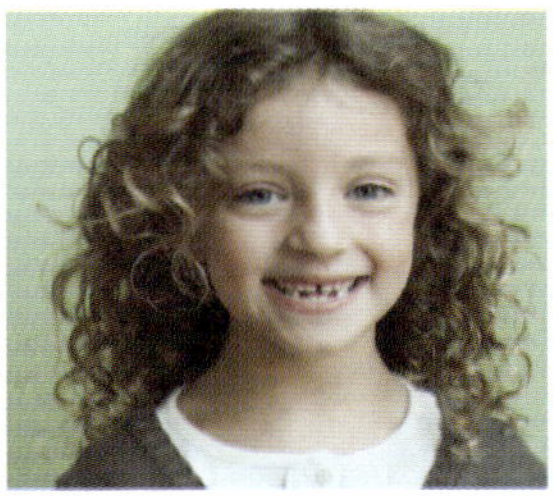
I'm happy.

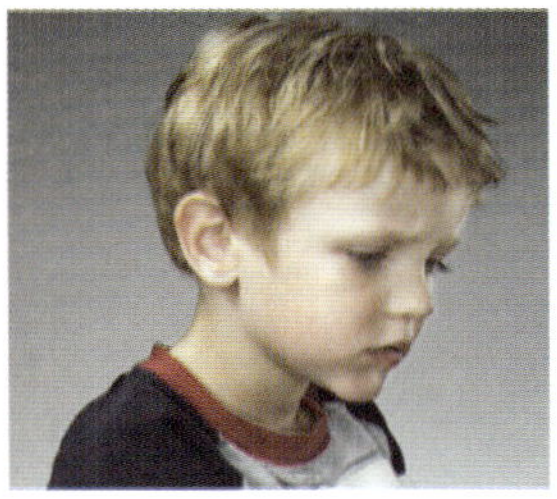
I'm sad.

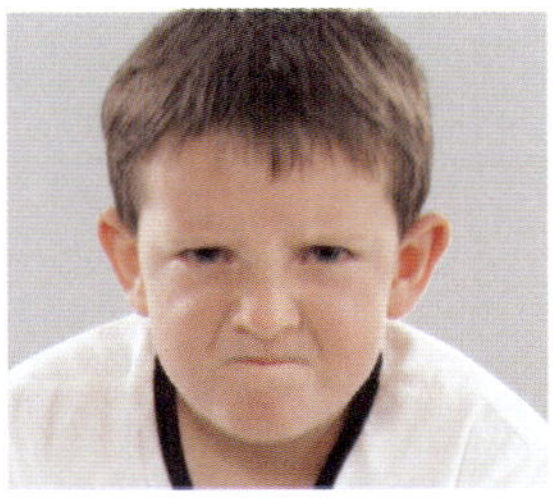
I'm angry.

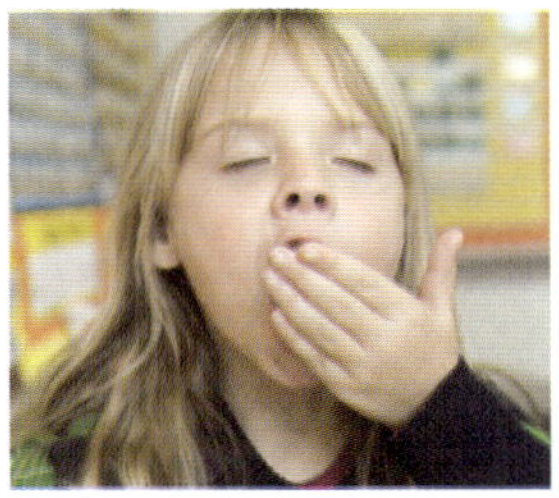
I'm tired.

2 Listen and read the rhyme. CD2 15

My feelings

When I'm sad,
I sit and cry.

When I'm happy,
I laugh and smile.

When I'm angry,
I stamp my feet.

When I'm tired,
I go to sleep.

3 **Cooperative learning:** Sing *We can do it!* CD2 16

4 Act out the rhyme.

After you read

Go to page 32 in your Activity Book.

1 Listen and number. Write and say.

CD2 17

fingers mouth ears nose eyes
legs ~~head~~ feet toes arms

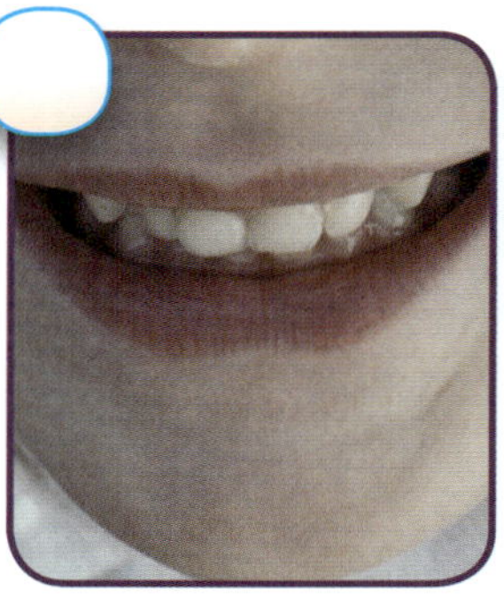

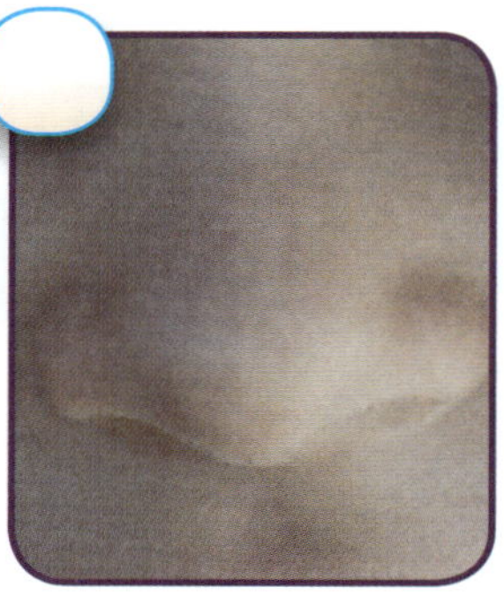

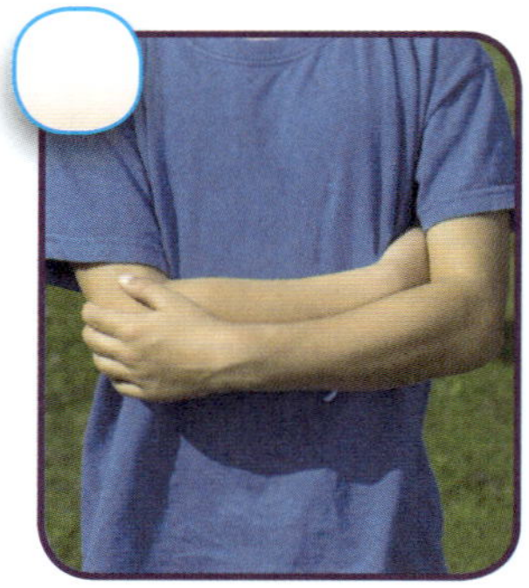

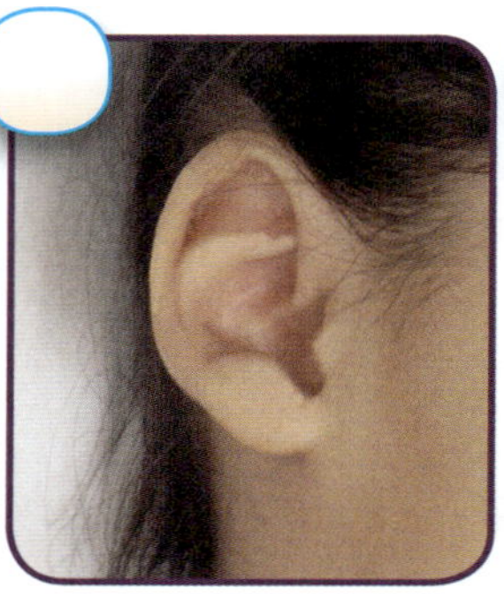

1 

head

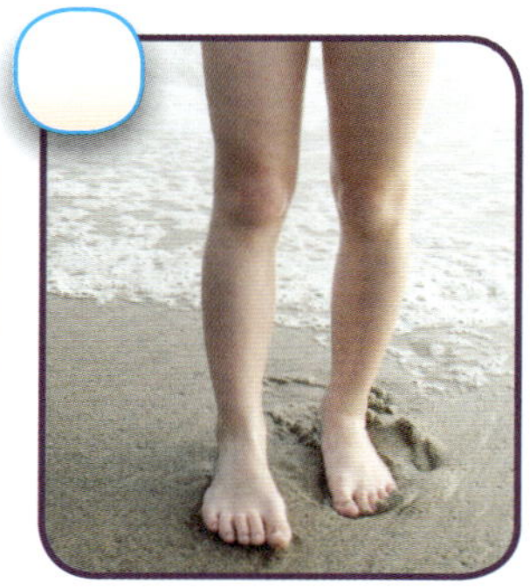

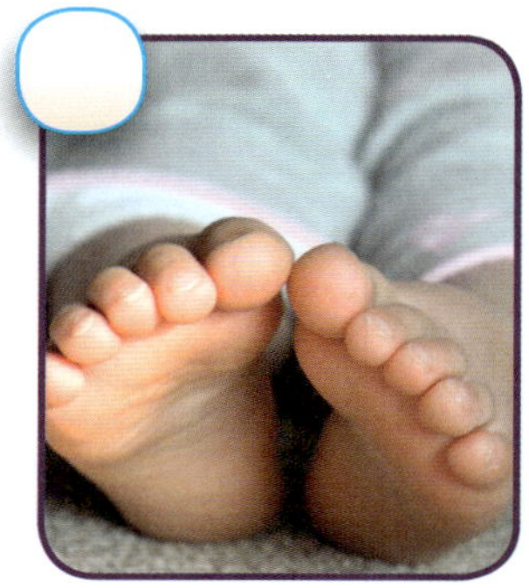

2 Read and write A or B.

1 She's got long hair. A
2 He's got short hair.
3 He's got brown eyes.
4 She's got green eyes.

3 Cooperative learning: Sing *Well done!*

CD2 18

HF External exams practice

1 Listen and tick (✓). There is one example.

CD2 19

1 Who is Ann?

A 
B 

2 Who is Tony?

A 
B 

3 Who is Ben?

A 
B 

4 Who is Kim?

A 
B 

2 Listen. Ask and answer.

CD2 20

Talk Partners

What colour is your hair?

My hair is black.

What colour are your eyes?

My eyes are brown.

My project 1: Family

Learn

1 Listen and point. Say. CD2 21

1 grandmother
2 grandfather
3 father
4 mother
5 uncle
6 aunt
7 brother
8 sister
9 cousins

Think

2 How many people are in your family? Think and colour.

brothers						
sisters						
aunts						
uncles						
cousins						

Vocabulary: family members

3 Listen. Ask and answer. Write the numbers.

CD2 22

Talk Partners

	brothers	sisters	aunts	uncles	cousins
me					
my friend					

4 Read, look and answer.

Have you got a big family?

Have you got a small family?

Plan your project

Prepare to make a family Christmas card. Go to page 36 in your Activity Book.

Language reinforcement and input: *Have you got (a brother)? Yes, I have. I've got (two brothers). / No, I haven't.*

Create

1 **Read. Make a family Christmas card.**

Show and tell

2 **Listen. Present your Christmas card.** CD2 23

Talk Partners

Language reinforcement and input: *This is my (mother). (Her) name is (Maria).*

Cooperative learning

3 Sing *It's fun to work together.* CD2 24

4 Make a class Christmas tree. Listen. Tell the class about your card. CD2 25

Think about your project Go to Page 37 in your Activity Book.

Language reinforcement and input:
This is my family. I've got a (small) family.

Unit 4

Lesson 1 Vocabulary

Fantastic food!

1 **Listen and point. Sing *Delicious food*.** CD2 26

I've got rice and eggs
And chicken today.
Delicious food
At the Astro Café!

I've got fish and chips
And salad today.
Delicious food
At the Astro Café!

I've got fruit and cake
And ice cream today.
Delicious food
At the Astro Café!

2 **Read and stick the ten stickers. Listen and say the chant.** CD2 28

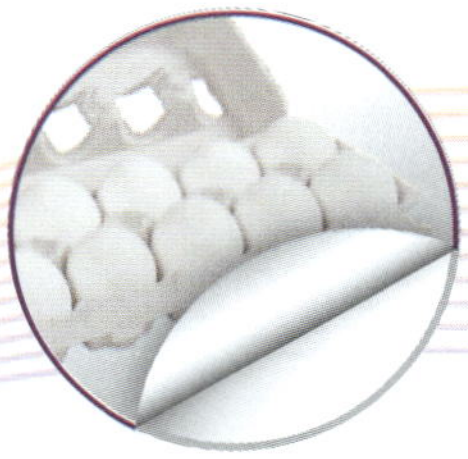

eggs

meat

fish

chips

rice

Vocabulary: food

Learning to LEARN

Spelling: Activity Book page 47

1 Listen and repeat. Act out.

CD2 29

Grammar

I like chicken.
I love ice cream.
I don't like fish.

2 Listen and draw a mouth.

CD2 30

love ☺ like ☺ don't like ☹

fruit cake salad chicken ice cream

Before you read What food can you see in the story?

1 **Listen and read. Act out.** CD2 31

I'm hungry

Language reinforcement and input:
I love cake. I don't like oranges. Do you like peaches? No, I don't.

High Five! values

2 **Read and circle.**

It's important to eat

ice cream / ***meat*** / ***fruit*** every day.

1 Listen, point and say. CD2 32

2 Listen and point. Sing *Do you like fruit?* CD2 33

I like grapes.
What about you?
Do you like grapes?
Do you like fruit?

I like grapes.
Yes, I do.
Eating fruit is fun to do.

I like peaches.
What about you?
Do you like peaches?
Do you like fruit?

I like peaches.
Yes, I do.
Eating fruit is fun to do.

3 Listen and repeat. Ask and answer. CD2 34

Do you like grapes?

Yes, I do. What about you?

No, I don't. I don't like grapes.

Vocabulary: fruit
Grammar: *Do you like (grapes)? Yes, I do. No, I don't.*

1 Listen and say. CD2 36

TOBY'S TONGUE TWISTER

j – j – j. Jim juggles jam, juice and jelly.

2 Listen and match. CD2 37

3 Make and play the game (Activity Book page 107).

4 **Cooperative learning:** Sing *Calm down*. CD2 38

British Culture

1 Listen and read. Answer. CD2 39

It's Sunday morning. Let's make a traditional English breakfast today.

1 Here are the ingredients: eggs, sausages, bacon, tomatoes and bread.

2 I mix the eggs. Lucy makes the toast. Dad cuts the tomatoes.

3 Dad cooks the food. We prepare the tray.

4 We take the breakfast to Mum. She's in bed. She's very happy.

Think about your culture **What do you have for breakfast?**

Literacy TEXT TYPE: A LUNCH MENU

Before you read

1 Read, look and circle.

1 How many days is the menu for?

a one day **b** three days **c** five days

2 Listen and read the lunch menu. CD2 41

Lunch Menu

Monday	Tuesday	Wednesday	Thursday	Friday
salad	carrots	soup	salad	soup
sausages and vegetables	chicken and pasta	meat and rice	chicken and potatoes	fish and salad
jelly	fruit	ice cream	fruit salad	carrot cake

After you read

Go to page 44 in your Activity Book.

1 Listen and number. Write and say. CD2 42

(1) meat · ______ · ______ · ______ · ______

______ · ______ · ______ · ______ · ______

______

2 Write about you. Complete the sentences.

1 I ______________________ salad.

2 I ______________________ eggs.

3 I ______________________ cake.

4 I ______________________.

5 I ______________________.

3 **Cooperative learning:** Sing *Well done!* CD2 43

HF External exams practice

1 Listen and tick (✓). There is one example. CD2 44

1 What is Bill's favourite food?

A

B

2 What is Lucy's favourite food?

A

B

3 What is Sue's favourite fruit?

A

B

4 What is Sam's favourite drink?

A

B

2 Listen. Ask and answer. CD2 45

Talk Partners

Fun on the farm

1 **Listen and point. Sing *On the farm*.** CD2 46

Animals, animals.
We love animals.
Animals, animals,
On the farm.

Can you see a duck?
Can you see a cat?
Yes, I can! Yes, I can!
The duck is yellow
And the cat is black.

Can you see a horse?
Can you see a cow?
Yes, I can! Yes, I can!
The horse is grey
And the cow is brown.

Can you see a sheep?
Can you see a pig?
Yes, I can! Yes, I can!
The sheep is white
And the pig is pink.

2 **Read and stick the ten stickers. Listen and say the chant.** CD2 48

cat cow bird frog goat

Vocabulary: farm animals

Learning to LEARN Spelling: Activity Book page 57

1 Listen and repeat. Act out. CD2 49

Grammar

Can you see Toby?
Yes, I can.
No, I can't.

2 Listen and colour the animals they can see. CD2 50

horse   sheep   duck   pig   chicken

Before you read

What animals can you see in the story?

1 Listen and read. Act out. CD2 51

Animal magic

Language reinforcement and input: *Cows can't fly. This sheep can climb trees. Can you see a cat? Yes, I can.*

High Five! values

2 Read and circle.

Remember! Wash your ***face*** / ***hands*** / ***feet*** after you touch animals.

1 Listen, point and say.

CD2 52

fly

swim

run

walk

climb

jump

2 Listen and point. Sing *Cats can't fly.*

CD2 53

I love cats.
Cats can fly.
No! No! No!
Cats can't fly.
Cats can climb.

I love frogs.
Frogs can run.
No! No! No!
Frogs can't run.
Frogs can jump.

I love cows.
Cows can talk.
No! No! No!
Cows can't talk.
Cows can walk.

3 Listen and repeat. Play a game.

CD2 54

Talk Partners

Vocabulary: actions
Grammar: *(Birds) can (fly). (Pigs) can't (climb).*

1 Listen and say. CD2 56

2 Listen. Tick or cross. can ✓ can't ✗ CD2 57

3 **Cooperative learning:** Sing *Let's take turns.* CD2 58

4 Make and play the game (Activity Book page 109).

Can you make 10 sentences?

British Culture

1 **Listen and read. Answer.** CD3 1

There's a farm in our town. Schools and families can visit the farm. It's very interesting.

1 I love the goats on the farm. I can feed them. Look. This goat is very hungry.

2 I love the horses. This horse is small and it's got lots of hair. Its name is Bob.

3 We can see chickens on the farm. I help the farmer to collect the eggs.

4 I like the garden. Fruit and vegetables grow here. Look. Here are some delicious carrots.

Think about your culture **Can you visit a farm in your country?**

Literacy

TEXT TYPE: ANIMAL RIDDLES

Before you read

1 Think and write a list with your partner.

Farm animals with two legs	Farm animals with four legs

2 Listen and read. Answer the riddles. CD3 3

Mrsgreenenglishclassblog

Fun zone | Homework zone | Class zone

Read the riddles. Can you guess the animals?

I've got two legs.
I can swim.
I can fly.
I'm small and brown.
What am I?

I've got four legs.
I can walk.
I can't climb.
I'm big.
I'm black and white.
What am I?

After you read

Go to page 54 in your Activity Book.

1 Listen and number. Write and say. CD3 4

1  chicken

 ______

 ______

 ______

 ______

 ______

 ______

 ______

 ______

 ______

2 Look at the pictures. Read and write the animal.

1 This animal can jump. It's green. frog
2 This animal can fly. It's black. ______
3 This animal can't fly. It's white. ______
4 This animal can swim. It's white. ______
5 This animal can climb. It's orange. ______
6 This animal can't swim. It's pink. ______

3 **Cooperative learning:** Sing *Well done!* CD3 5

HF External exams practice

1 Listen and tick (✓). There is one example.

CD3 6

1 What can Peter see?

A

B

2 What can Sally see?

A

B

3 What can Emma see?

A

B

4 What can Alex see?

A

B

2 Listen. Ask and answer.

CD3 7

Talk Partners

jump swim walk juggle fly climb run ride a bike

A day in the park

1 **Listen and point. Sing** *It's fun in the park.* CD3 8

We can climb a tree.
We can jump and run.
We can play on the swing.
The park is fun.

It's fun, fun, fun in the park.
Yes, it's fun, fun, fun in the park.

We can play on the slide.
We can jump and run.
We can play on the roundabout.
The park is fun.

Chorus

We can play on the grass.
We can jump and run.
We can play on the seesaw.
The park is fun.

Chorus

2 **Read and stick the ten stickers. Listen and say the chant.** CD3 10

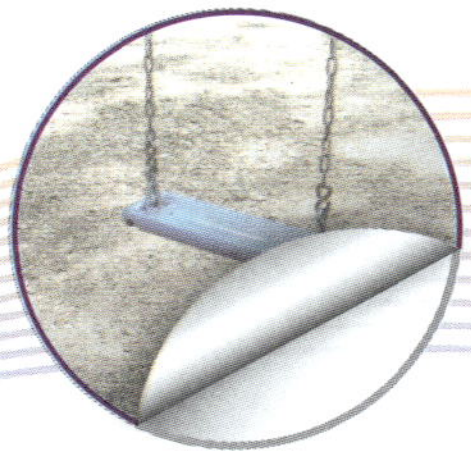

swing

slide

seesaw

roundabout

climbing frame

Vocabulary: playground objects and nature

Learning to LEARN

Spelling: Activity Book page 67

1 Listen and repeat. Act out.

CD3 11

Grammar

Where's my sister?
She's on the swing.
Where's my brother?
He's on the roundabout.

2 Listen and match.

CD3 12

1 

2 

3 

4 

a 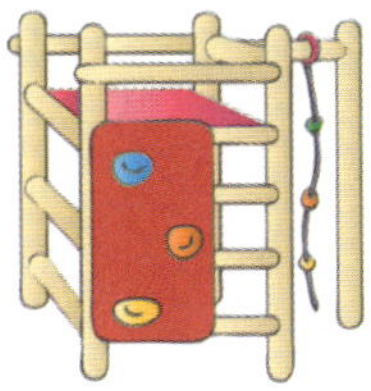

b 

c 

d 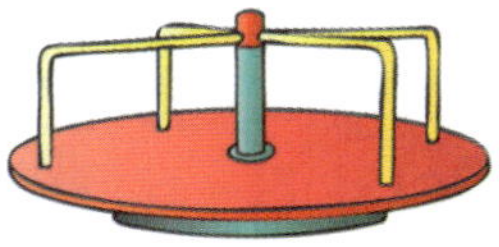

grass flower tree bush rock

Before you read

What can you see in the playground?

1 Listen and read. Act out.

CD3 13

Language reinforcement and input: *Where's Toby? He's on the slide. Where are Jake and Molly? They're behind the tree.*

High Five! values

2 **Read and circle.**

Remember! ***Respect*** / ***Write*** / ***Say*** the signs around you.

1 Listen, point and say.

CD3 14

behind the tree | near the grass | in front of the flowers | next to the bush | between the rocks

2 Listen and point. Sing *Hide and seek*.

CD3 15

Hide, hide,
Hide everyone.
Ready or not,
Here I come!

Where are Jake and Molly?
Where are they?
They're next to the tree.
Let's play again!

Where are Beth and Molly?
Where are they?
They're near the rocks.
Let's play again!

Where are Jake and Beth?
Where are they?
They're behind the bush.
Let's play again!

3 Listen and repeat. Ask and answer.

CD3 16

Talk Partners

Vocabulary: prepositions
Grammar: *Where are (Jake and Molly)? They're (next to the tree).*

TOBY'S TONGUE TWISTER

1 Listen and say. CD3 18

2 Listen and match. CD3 19

1

2

3

4

3 **Cooperative learning:** Sing *Listen to others*. CD3 20

4 Make and play the game (Activity Book page 109).

British Culture

1 Listen and read. Answer. CD3 21

I love the park in my town. It's very big.
I go with my family on Saturday.
We do lots of fun activities.

1 We play cricket on the grass. Look. I can hit the ball.

2 We feed the ducks on the pond. They love bread.

3 We ride on the train. It's great!

4 We love the playground. The zip wire is very fast.

Think about your culture What do you do at the park?

Literacy TEXT TYPE: INSTRUCTIONS

Before you read

1 What do you need to grow flowers? Think and circle.

soil

grass

a book

seeds

water

sun

2 Listen and read the instructions. CD3 23

My garden

Pansy

Ask an adult to help you. Do not eat seeds.

Instructions

1 Put the soil in a pot.

2 Push the seeds into the soil with your finger.

3 Water the seeds.

4 Put the pot in a sunny place. Watch the plants grow.

5 Put the plants in the garden. Watch the flowers grow.

After you read

Go to page 64 in your Activity Book.

1 **Listen and number. Write and say.** CD3 24

1

______ swing ______ ______ ______

______ ______ ______ ______ ______

______

2 **Look, read and write.**

in front of *next to* *behind*

1 Where's Toby? He's ______ a rock.

2 Where's Molly? She's ______ a bush.

3 Where are Beth and Jake? They're ______ a rock.

3 **Cooperative learning:** Sing *Well done!* CD3 25

HF External exams practice

1 Listen and colour. There is one example. CD3 26

2 Listen. Ask and answer. CD3 27 Talk Partners

My project 2: Spring

Remember and learn

1 **Listen and say. Find, count and write.** CD3 28

3 lambs	flowers	birds
rabbits	trees	butterflies
chicks	bushes	

2 **Listen. Ask and answer.** CD3 29 Talk Partners

Vocabulary: spring animals and plants
Language reinforcement and input: *How many (flowers) can you see? I can see (seven flowers).*

Learn

3 **Listen and point. Say.** CD3 30

It's sunny.

It's windy.

It's rainy.

It's cloudy.

It's snowy.

It's stormy.

4 **Listen. Ask and answer.** CD3 31

Plan your project

➔ **Prepare to make a spring wall display. Go to page 68 in your Activity Book.**

Language input: *What's the weather like today? It's (windy). Is it (rainy) today? Yes, it is. No, it isn't.*

Create

1 **Cooperative learning:** Sing *What do I need to do?* CD3 32

2 Read. Make a spring animal.

1

Cut out your spring animal.
Be careful with the scissors!

2

Make balls with the tissue paper.
Use different colours.

3

Stick the balls on your spring animal.

Show and tell

3 Listen. Tell your partner about your animal. CD3 33 Talk Partners

Language reinforcement and input: *This is my (rabbit). It's (brown, pink and white). It's got (big ears).*

Cooperative learning

4 Paint your wall display.

5 Stick your spring animals on the wall display.

6 Listen. Ask and answer. CD3 34 Talk Partners

Think about your project Go to Page 69 in your Activity Book.

Language reinforcement and input: *How many (flowers) can you see? I can see (three flowers). Where's the (blue flower)? It's (between) the (chick) and the (rabbit).*

Unit 7

Lesson 1 Vocabulary

Let's explore my town!

1 **Listen and point. Sing *Let's go to town*.** CD3 35

Stand up.
Sit down.
Let's go to town
To see what we can see.

There's a cinema.
There's a bookshop, too.
There's a hospital
And there's a swimming pool.

Chorus

There's a supermarket.
There's a sweet shop, too.
There's a restaurant.
And look! There's a zoo!

Chorus

2 **Read and stick the ten stickers. Listen and say the chant.** CD3 37

zoo | sweet shop | café | toyshop | bookshop

Vocabulary: places in the town

Learning to LEARN

Spelling: Activity Book page 79

1 Listen and repeat. Act out.

CD3 38

Grammar

There's a zoo.
There are two sweet shops.

2 How many are there? Listen and write the number.

CD3 39

2

hospital   restaurant   cinema   swimming pool   supermarket

Before you read

What places can you see in the story?

1 Listen and read. Act out.

CD3 40

The treasure hunt

Language reinforcement and input: *There's a tree next to the swimming pool. There are two rocks in front of the zoo. How many steps are there?*

5

6

7

8

High Five! values

2 Read and write.

red *yellow* *green*

Remember! Cross the road when the man is ______________.

1 Listen, point and say.

CD3 41

bus

boat

motorbike

train

helicopter

lorry

2 Listen and point. Sing *How many?*

CD3 42

Ready, Steady, Go!

How many? How many?
How many cars are there?

One, two, three,
Four, five, six,
Seven, eight cars.

Nine, ten,
Eleven, twelve,
Thirteen, fourteen cars

Fifteen, sixteen,
Seventeen, eighteen,
Nineteen, twenty cars.

There are twenty cars.
Yes, there are twenty cars.

3 Listen and repeat. Play a memory game.

CD3 43

Talk Partners

How many motorbikes are there?

There are 15 motorbikes.

Correct!

Vocabulary: transport; numbers 11–20
Grammar: *How many (cars) are there?*

1 Listen and say. CD3 45

2 Listen and cross out the transport. Say *Bingo*. CD3 46

3 Make the cards. Play *Bingo* (Activity Book page 111).

British Culture

1 **Listen and read. Answer.** CD3 47

Lots of people travel by bike in our town. Cycling is fun and it's good exercise, too. We love our bikes!

1 On Monday, there's a cycling class in the school playground.

2 On Saturday, we go shopping. We go to the town centre by bike with Mum.

3 This is a rickshaw. It's got three wheels. You can see our town in a rickshaw. There are lots of things to see!

4 There are lots of bikes in our town. Oh no! Where's my bike?

Think about your culture **How do you travel in your town?**

Literacy TEXT TYPE: A FABLE

Before you read

1 Where do you think the mice live? Write. *town country*

I live in the ________________.

I live in the ________________.

2 Listen and read the fable. CD3 49

Town Mouse and Country Mouse

Town Mouse travels to the country. He visits his cousin, Country Mouse. They eat cheese and apples.

Country Mouse travels to the town with his cousin, Town Mouse. They eat chocolate cake and ice cream.

Suddenly, Country Mouse hears a noise.

Country Mouse is scared. He runs and he runs and he runs. Soon, he is in the country again.

After you read

Go to page 76 in your Activity Book.

1 Listen and number. Write and say. CD3 50

1 

______ restaurant ______ ______ ______

______ ______ ______ ______ ______

______

2 What can you see in your classroom? Read, count and answer.

1 How many boards are there?

There ______________________.

2 How many bins are there?

There ______________________.

3 How many cupboards are there?

There ______________________.

3 **Cooperative learning:** Sing *Well done!* CD3 51

HF External exams practice

1 Listen and tick (✓). There is one example.

CD3 52

1 Where is Nick?

A

B

2 Where is Jill?

A

B

3 Where is Bill?

A

B

4 Where is Jane?

A

B

2 Listen. Ask and answer.

CD3 53

Talk Partners

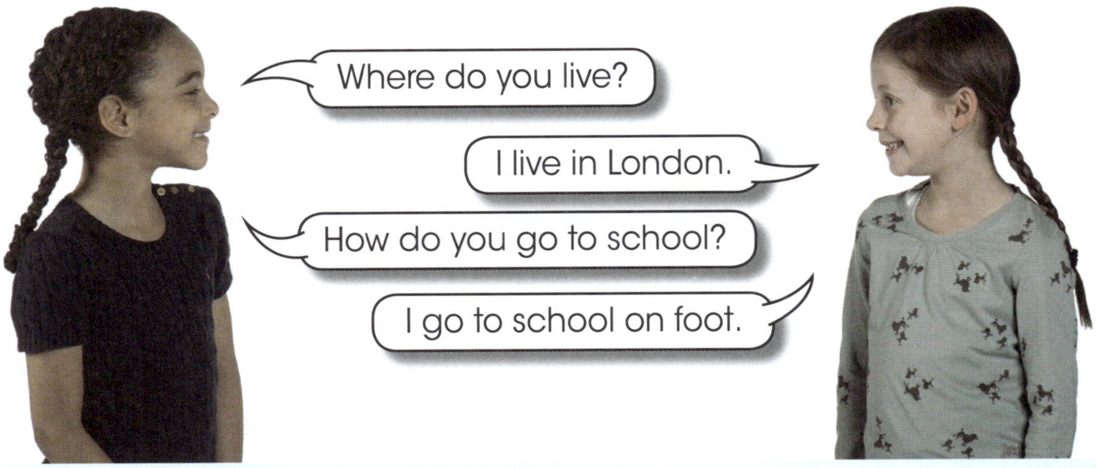

by bike | by car | by bus | on the metro | on foot

Unit 8 Lesson 1 Vocabulary

Camping fun!

1 Listen and point. Sing *What are you wearing?*

CD4 1

What are you wearing?
Hey! Hey! Hey!
What are you wearing today?

I'm wearing shorts
And a T-shirt, too.
I'm wearing a sun hat.
What about you?

Chorus

I'm wearing a shirt
And trousers, too.
I'm wearing trainers.
What about you?

Chorus

I'm wearing a skirt
And a sweater, too.
I'm wearing shoes.
What about you?

Chorus

2 Read and stick the ten stickers. Listen and say the chant.

CD4 3

sweater

shoes

T-shirt

skirt

sun hat

Vocabulary: clothes

Learning to LEARN

Spelling: Activity Book page 89

1 Listen and repeat. Act out.

CD4 4

Grammar

What are you wearing?
I am wearing a T-shirt.
I'm wearing a T-shirt.

2 Listen and match.

CD4 5

trainers shirt swimsuit shorts trousers

Before you read

What's the weather like in the story?

1 Listen and read. Act out. CD4 6

Fun at the camp

Language reinforcement and input: *I'm wearing trousers. She's riding a horse. He's sailing a boat.*

High Five! values

2 Read and write.

red yellow green

Don't go in the water when the flag is __________________. It's dangerous.

Lesson 4 Vocabulary and Grammar

1 Listen, point and say.

CD4 7

sail a boat

ride a horse

play the guitar

play volleyball

sing songs

2 Listen and point. Sing *Camping is great!*

CD4 8

We're in a forest
Near a lake.
Camping is great.
Yes! Camping is great!

What's Molly doing in the sun?
She's riding a horse.
She's having fun!

What's Beth doing in the sun?
She's sailing a boat.
She's having fun!

What's Jake doing in the sun?
He's playing the guitar.
He's having fun!

3 Listen and repeat. Play a game.

CD4 9

Talk Partners

Vocabulary: outdoor activities
Grammar: *What's he / she doing? He's / She's (playing the guitar).*

1 Listen and say. CD4 11

TOBY'S TONGUE TWISTER

v – v – v. Vicky the vet loves volleyball.

2 Listen and match. CD4 12

1 Emma

2 Ben

3 Tom

4 Susan

5 Alex

6 Mary

3 Make and play the game (Activity Book page 111).

British Culture

1 **Listen and read. Answer.** CD4 13

In the summer, we camp in the garden. It's good fun.

1 Dad plays the guitar, and we sing songs. My favourite song is 'Alice the camel'. It's funny.

2 We sleep in our sleeping bags in a big tent.

3 At night, we tell ghost stories. They're scary!

2 **Listen and sing** ***Alice the camel*****.** CD4 14

Alice the camel has five humps.
Alice the camel has five humps.
Alice the camel has five humps.

So go, Alice, go!
BOOM! BOOM! BOOM!

Alice the camel has four humps …
Alice the camel has three humps …
Alice the camel has two humps …
Alice the camel has one hump …
Alice the camel has no humps …
Now Alice is a horse!

Think about your culture **Do you go camping? What activities do you do?**

Literacy TEXT TYPE: A POSTCARD

Before you read

1 What can you see on the postcard? Circle and say.

a town
a lake
a playground
boats
a forest
horses
a farm

2 Listen and read the postcard. CD4 16

Dear Sally,

I'm at a fantastic campsite with my family. There's a beautiful forest and there's a big lake. There are lots of fun activities here. I swim in the lake and I sail a boat every day.

It's hot and sunny today. I'm wearing my new swimsuit. It's purple and pink.

See you soon,

Sue

Sally Smith
12 Park Street
London
NE14 6TN

After you read

Go to page 86 in your Activity Book.

1 Listen and number. Write and say.

CD4 17

______ ______ ______ ______ ______

1

______ ______ T-shirt ______ ______

2 Look, read and complete.

3 Cooperative learning: Sing *Well done!*

CD4 18

HF External exams practice

1 Listen and tick (✓). There is one example. CD4 19

1 What is Bill wearing?

A 

B 

2 What is May wearing?

A 

B 

3 What is Nick doing?

A 

B 

4 What is Jill doing?

A 

B 

2 Listen. Ask and answer. CD4 20

Talk Partners

Day and night

1 Listen and do the actions. Sing *It's a beautiful day*. CD4 21

I get up.
I get dressed.
I open the window and I say
It's a beautiful day.
It's a beautiful day today.

I wash my face.
I brush my teeth.
I open the window and I say
It's a beautiful day.
It's a beautiful day today.

I comb my hair.
I make my bed.
I open the window and I say
It's a beautiful day.
It's a beautiful day today.

2 Read and stick the ten stickers. Listen and say the chant. CD4 23

get up

wash my face

brush my teeth

comb my hair

have a shower

Vocabulary: daily routines

Learning to LEARN

Spelling: Activity Book page 99

1 Listen and repeat. Act out.

CD4 24

Grammar

I wash my face every day.
Me, too.

2 Listen and tick (✓).

CD4 25

	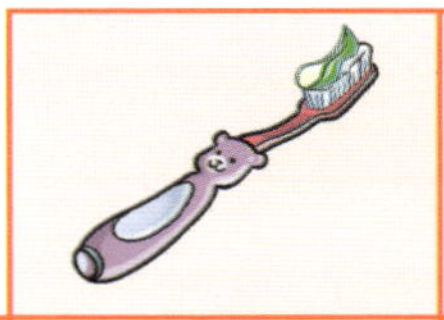					
1 	✓					
2 						

get dressed | make my bed | go to school | go to bed | sleep

Before you read

1 **Listen and read. Act out.** CD4 26

The wobbly tooth

Language reinforcement and input:
I have breakfast every morning.

5

6

7 After dinner ...

8

High Five! values

2 Read and write.

teeth   feet   hands

Remember! Brush your ___________
before you go to bed.

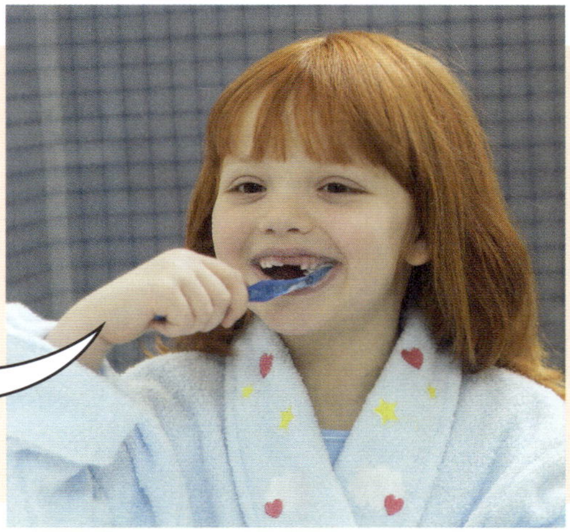

9 Lesson 4 Vocabulary and Grammar

1 Listen, point and say. CD4 27

breakfast in the morning

lunch in the afternoon

dinner in the evening

a snack at night

2 Listen and point. Sing *Are you hungry?* CD4 28

Are you hungry in the morning?
Yes, I am. Yes, I am.
I have breakfast in the morning.
Yum, yum, yum.

Are you hungry in the afternoon?
Yes, I am. Yes, I am.
I have lunch in the afternoon.
Yum, yum, yum.

Are you hungry in the evening?
Yes, I am. Yes, I am.
I have dinner in the evening.
Yum, yum, yum.

3 Listen and repeat. Play a game. CD4 29

Talk Partners

Vocabulary: meal times
Grammar: *I have (dinner in the evening).*

1 Listen and say. CD4 31

TOBY'S TONGUE TWISTER

th – th – th. Three thin tigers have a bath on Thursday.

2 Listen and match. CD4 32

1 

2 

3 

at night

in the evening

in the morning

3 Make and play the game (Activity Book page 113).

British Culture

1 Listen and read. Answer. CD4 33

In Britain, the Tooth Fairy visits children's bedrooms at night.

1 When my tooth falls out, I put it in a box. I put the box under my pillow.

2 The Tooth Fairy comes at night. She takes my tooth when I'm sleeping.

3 In the morning, I find a letter from the Tooth Fairy. The letter says 'Thank you, Lucy'.

4 I find money from the Tooth Fairy, too. I put it in my piggy bank.

Think about your culture **Have you got a Tooth Fairy in your country?**

Literacy TEXT TYPE: A POEM

Before you read

1 Listen and number. Say *day* or *night*. CD4 34

sleep

owl

cockerel

children

2 Listen and read the poem. CD4 35

Morning time

It's morning time.
The sun is in the sky.
The moon and the stars
Say goodbye.

The owl goes to sleep
With a whoo whoo.
And the cockerel crows
Cock-a-doodle-doo.

Get up, children
It's a new day.
Get up, children
It's time to play.

3 Act out the poem.

After you read

Go to page 96 in your Activity Book.

1 Listen and number. Write and say.

CD4 37

1

sleep

2 Look and write.

evening night ~~morning~~ afternoon

1

morning

2

3

4

3 **Cooperative learning:** Sing *Well done!*

CD4 38

HF External exams practice

1 Listen and tick (✓). There is one example. CD4 39

1 Which is Ben's breakfast?

A  ✓

B 

2 Who is Jill?

A 

B 

3 Who is Tom?

A 

B 

4 Who is Ann?

A 

B 

2 Listen. Ask and answer. CD4 40

Talk Partners

What do you do in the morning?

I have breakfast.

What do you have for breakfast?

I have cereal and milk.

My project 3: Holidays

Learn

1 Listen, point and say. Tick (✓) your favourite place for a holiday. CD4 41

beach

mountains

country

jungle

desert

city

2 Listen. Ask and answer. CD4 42 Talk Partners

Vocabulary: places for a holiday
Language reinforcement and input: *What's your favourite place? My favourite place is (the beach).*

Remember and learn

3 Listen, point and say. CD4 43

map

boots

water

swimsuit

sunglasses

sweets

camera

torch

4 Listen. Play the holiday game. CD4 44 Talk Partners

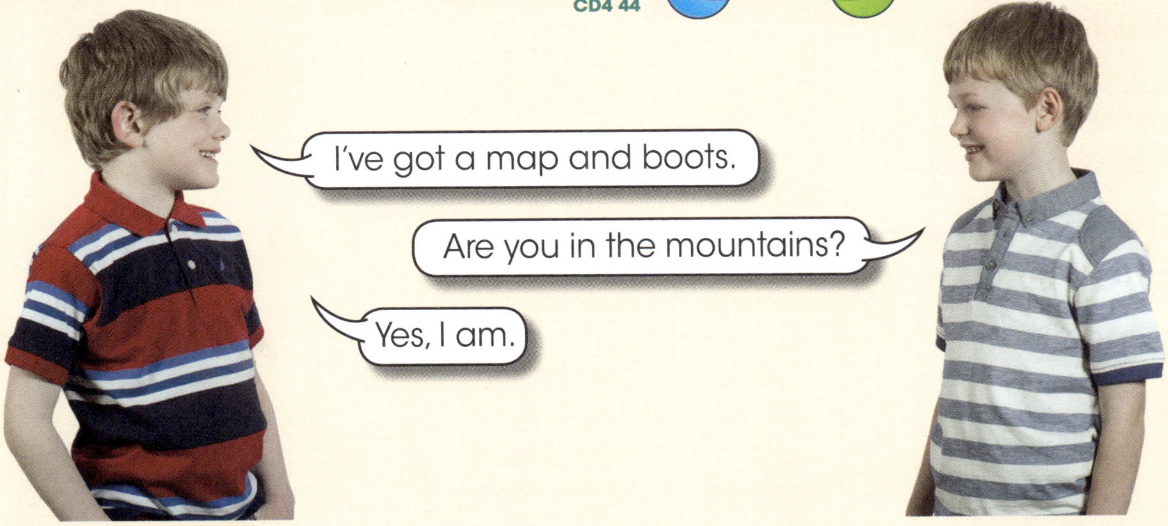

Plan your project

➔ **Prepare to make a holiday poster. Go to page 100 in your Activity Book.**

Create

1 Read. Make your model.

1

2

3

Show and tell

2 Listen. Tell your partner about you. CD4 45 Talk Partners

Language reinforcement: *I'm wearing (red trousers). There's (a map and a swimsuit) in my rucksack.*

Cooperative learning

3 Sing *Sharing is a good thing to do.* CD4 46

4 Make a group holiday poster.

1

Draw your favourite holiday place. Decorate your poster.

2

Stick your people on the poster.

Show and tell

5 Listen. Present your poster to the class. CD4 47 Talk Partners

Think about your work Go to page 101 in your Activity Book.

Language reinforcement: *She's wearing (a yellow T-shirt). There's (a camera) in her rucksack.*

Festivals

Christmas

1 Listen. Find and count. Sing *Merry Christmas*.

CD4 48

Merry Christmas.
Merry Christmas.
Ho! Ho! Ho! Ho! Ho!

I'm Father Christmas.
I've got some toys.
I give them to the girls and boys.

Chorus

Look at the presents
Under the tree.
One for you and one for me!

Chorus

1  Father Christmas

 presents

 stars

 Christmas tree

 stockings

2 Listen and match.

CD4 49

Think about your culture

Who brings presents in your country?

Make a Christmas stocking. Go to pages 115 and 116 in your Activity Book.

Language input: *What do you want for Christmas?*
Can I have (a train), please?

Easter

1 Read and listen. CD4 50

British children do fun activities at Easter. You can try one of these activities at school or at home.

1 We make special Easter hats at school. We wear our hats in an Easter hat parade.

2 We decorate eggs. Look, a butterfly and a bird.

3 We look for Easter eggs in the garden. It's fun!

2 Listen and number. CD4 51

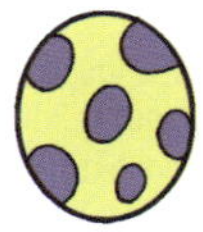

spots

zigzags

Make an Easter card. Go to pages 117 and 118 in your Activity Book.

Think about your culture

What activities do you do at Easter?

Macmillan Education
4 Crinan Street
London
N1 9XW

A division of Macmillan Publishers Limited
Companies and representatives throughout the world

ISBN 978-0-230-42697-9
Pack ISBN 978-0-230-46393-6

First published 2014

Series concept design by Tom Cole
Designed by Anthony Godber
Illustrated by Ángeles Peinador, Jorge Santillan, Eric Smith, Adrian Barclay, Clive Goodyer, Matt Ward, Tony De Saulles, Sholto Walker, Sam Church, Laszlo Veres, Julia Patton, Kathy Baxendale
Cover design by Bigtop Design Limited
Cover images by Alamy/BL Images Ltd, Alamy/Bozena Fulawka, Alamy/Anna Omelchenko, Getty/André Thijssen, Macmillan Publishers Ltd/Lisa Payne
Course consultants: Rocío Gutiérrez Burgos and Mónica Pérez Is
Pictures researched by Sally Cole
Songs produced and arranged by Tom, Dick and Debbie Productions
Recordings produced and arranged by Footstep Productions

Authors' acknowledgements
The authors would like to thank everyone at Macmillan who has given help and advice throughout this project. Special thanks from Jo to Carlos, Daniel and Alex for their patience and support during this process. Special thanks from Donna to José, Elisa, Teresa and Marina for their encouragement and enthusiasm.

Acknowledgements
The publishers would like to thank the following teachers for their contribution to the project:
Amanda Morrison Prince, Colegio El Parque, La Navata, Madrid; Amaya Carrera García, Colegio Santa Teresa de Jesús, Valladolid; Ana Isabel Fernández Sáez, CEIP La Encina, Las Rozas, Madrid; Aránzazu Sánchez Rodríguez, CEIP Rosa Luxemburgo, Madrid; Beatriz García Vaquero, CEIP Mariano José de Larra, Madrid; Carme Tena, Col·legi Sagrada Familia, Tortosa, Tarragona; Carmen María Largo Muñoz, CEIP Federico García Lorca, Colmenar Viejo, Madrid; Cristina Nieto Ruíz de Gaona, CEIP Margarita Salas, Arroyo de la Encomienda, Valladolid; Estíbaliz Medina Martín, CEIP Virgen de Navalazarza, San Agustín de Guadalix, Madrid; Iratxe Zabaleta Zendagorta, Ikastola San Fidel, Guernica, Vizcaya; Lucía Manso Estébanez, CEIP Ciudad de Guadalajara, Madrid; Lucía López Sánchez, CEIP San Juan de la Cruz, Madrid; Lucía Soria García, CEIP Alberto Alcocer, Madrid; Marta Moreno Arroyo, CEIP Vicente Aleixandre, Móstoles, Madrid; Susana Espinel Beneitez, Colegio Grazalema, El Puerto de Santa María, Cádiz; Susana García Pizarro, Ateneu Instructiu, Sant Joan Despí, Barcelona; Virginia Escalona Monreal, CEIP La Encina, Las Rozas, Madrid.

The authors and publishers would like to thank the following for permission to reproduce their photographs:
Alamy/amphotos p49(chicken & potatoes), Alamy/A.Amsel p84(café), Alamy/Y.Arcurs p79(br), Alamy/Art Directors & Trip p86, 94(sweater), Alamy/Blend Images p36(fingers), Alamy/N.Bilic p49(chicken & pasta), Alamy/P. Bonek pp26, 110(train), Alamy/D.Bronze p16(sharpener), Alamy/Catchlight Visual Services p32(blonde hair), Alamy/N.Cattlin p59(cow), Alamy/R. Coombs p65(br), Alamy/Cultura Creative p55(br), Alamy/V.Dobosh pp62(bl), 70(swing), Alamy/M.Dyball p80(boat), Alamy/C.Eckert pp76, 84(zoo), Alamy/G.Balfour Evans p84(restaurant), Alamy/Eye Stock p107(boots), Alamy/Food & Drink Photos p59(hen), Alamy/Format4 p80(bus), Alamy/I. Fraser pp82(t), 83(t), Alamy/Y.Gapeenko p94(shoes), Alamy/V.Gudovskiy p49(salad), Alamy/E.Hiltula p70(roundabout), Alamy/D.Hurst pp12(board), 26(kite), Alamy/imagebroker p56(climb), Alamy/incamerastock pp50(meat), 70(slide), 70(climbing frame), Alamy/Juniors Bildarchiv Gmbh p90(riding), Alamy/C.Kennedy p104(comb), Alamy/R.Kudrin p94(shirt), Alamy/A.Kuzmin p16(ruler), Alamy.D.Lee p49(meat & rice), Alamy/I.Leonard p26(computer game), Alamy/Metta foto p107(sunglasses), Alamy/MBI p45(br), Alamy/D. Green-Nature p73(storm), Alamy/J.Norman p80(train), Alamy/P.Oshkai p70(rock), Alamy/C.Pearsall p79(br), Alamy/PetStock Boys p60(chicken), Alamy/J.Pham Photography p12(cupboard), Alamy/Redfx p12(chair), Alamy/G. Roebuck p36(toes), Alamy/A.Sadovskiy p94(trousers), Alamy/G.Samoylovich p104(shower), Alamy/D.Schneider p65(br), Alamy/A.Segre p84(supermarket), Alamy/L.Serebrennikov p70(flower), Alamy/A.Starikov p94(skirt), Alamy/Steppenwolf p84(pool), Alamy/SugarStock Ltd p49(salad), Alamy/T.M.O. Pictures p90(sailing), Alamy/J.T.Turner p73(snow), Alamy/A.Ugorenkov pp26, 110(dinosaur), Alamy/V.Volkov p107(water), Alamy/T.Wang p12(desk), Alamy/Wavebreak Media Ltd p39(br), Alamy/D.White p89(br), Alamy/Whitebox Media Ltd p49(sausage), Alamy/J.Kase zsixz p80(lorry); **Bananastock** pp28(bl), 36 (mouth), (nose), (head), (eyes), 104(sleeping), 107(sweets); **Corbis** p70(grass), 73(cloud), Corbis/AStock p70(seesaw), Corbis/BDLM/Cultura p32(brown hair), Corbis/Blend Images pp90(guitar), 104(bed), Corbis/R.Landau p70(bush), Corbis/Loop Images p84(bookshop), Corbis/Minden Pictures p106(jungle), Corbis/Ocean pp26(scooter), 69(seeds), 107(camera), 107(map), 17(t), 27(t), 37(t), 51(t), 61(t), 71(t), 85(t), 95(t), 105(t), Corbis/D.Selman p46(grape), Corbis/Z.Seckler p70(tree), Corbis/A.Skelley p99(br), Corbis/TongRo Images p56(walk), Corbis/B.Wood p56(run); **Comstock Images** pp46(cherry), 50(salad); **Fancy** pp58(t), 59(t); **FLPA**/D.Hosking p60(frog), FLPA/G.Lacz p56(jump), FLPA/N.Bowman p60(bird); **Fotolibra**/N.Jenkins p84(sweetshop), Fotolibra/Petejeff p106(rural); **Getty RF** pp12(bin), 16(bag), 16(computer), 18, 26(ball), 46(mango), (peach), (lemon), 50(ice cream), 50(rice), 106(desert); **Getty Images**/Blend Images pp32(short hair), 35(happy), 90(singing), Getty Images/BrandX Pictures p35(tired),Getty Images/Dorling Kindersley pp26(car), 26, 110(doll), 49(soup), 50(fish), 60(pig), 60(horse), 69(soil), 69(water), Getty Images/E+ pp49(cake), 60(cow), 60(goat), 94(shoes), 111(c), Getty Images/F1online p59(bird), Getty Images/Flickr pp36(legs), 104(walking), Getty Images/Flickr Select p39(bl), Getty Images/Foodpix p50(chicken), Getty Images/Iconica p69(grass), Getty Images/Imagebank p21(br), Getty Images/Imagesource p80(helicopter), Getty Images/OJO Images p106(mountains), Getty Images/Photoalto Agency p90(volleyball), Getty Images/Photographers Choice p69(bl), Getty Images/Photolibrary pp49(jelly), 50(chips), 93(r), Getty Images/Stone pp38, p104(getting dressed); **Image100** p36(ears); **Image Source** pp50(cake), 84(cinema), 104(brushing teeth), 107(sweets); **John Foxx Images** pp56(fly), 59(dog), 60(sheep), 60(duck); **Macmillan Publishers Ltd**/P.Bricknell pp8, 16, 69(book), 16(pen), 16(rubber), 26, 110(teddy), 94(hat), 104(washing), Macmillan Publishers/P.Bricknell & D.Ryan p49(soup), Macmillan Publishers Ltd/H.Davies pp16(pencil case), 94(shorts), Macmillan Publishers Ltd/R.Judges/D.Dubber p107(torch), Macmillan Publishers Ltd/L.Payne pp16(pencil), 16(crayon), Macmillan Publishers Ltd/D.Ryan/R.Judges p12(shelf), Macmillan Publishers Ltd/D.Tolley pp94(t-shirt), 107(swimsuit); **Photodisc** pp42(eggs), 46(coconut), (salad x2), p50(fruit), 106(beach); **Photospin** pp52, 60(cat); **Plainpicture**/Beyond p59(horse), Plainpicture/Elektrons 08 p73(wind), Plainpicture/Folio Images p35(sad), Plainpicture/Glasshouse p106(city), Plainpicture/OJO pp48(t), 49(t), Plainpicture/H.Sauber pp68(t), 69(t), Plainpicture/Stock4B p36(feet); **Shutterstock** pp24(t), 25(t); **Stockbyte** p26(robot); **Superstock**/All Canada Photos p59(duck), Superstock/Blend Images pp32(long hair), 104(bedtime), 111(r), Superstock/ClassicStock.com p32(red hair), Superstock/Corbis pp96(bl), 104, Superstock/Cultura Ltd p36(arms), Superstock/F1online p84(hospital), Superstock/Flirt pp34(t), 35(t), 73(rain), Superstock/Food & Drink pp49(fruit), (fish & salad), Superstock/Fotosearch p35(angry), Superstock/imagebroker.net p56(swim), Superstock/Photosindia.com p32(black hair), Superstock/Pixtal p69(sun), Superstock/Purestock p49(fruit salad), Superstock/Radius p73(sun), Superstock/Stock Connection pp31(br), 80(motorbike), Superstock/Tips Images p49(ice cream), Superstock/Universal Images Group p111(l), Superstock/S. Vidler p84(toyshop).

Photographs re-used on stickers:
Alamy; Bananastock; Comstock Images; Corbis; FLPA; Fotolibra; Getty, Image100; Image Source; John Foxx Images; Macmillan Publishers Ltd; Photospin; Photodisc; Plainpicture; Stockbyte; Superstock.

Commissioned photography by Lisa Payne pp7,11(bl), 12,13,14,16(br),17, 21(bl),22,23,24,26(br),27,31(bl),32,33,34,36(br),37,39(t),40,41,45(bl), 46(b),47(b),48,50(br),51,55(bl),56(b),57(b),58,60(br),61,65(bl),66,67,68, 70(br),71,72,73,74,75,79(bl),81,82,84(br),85,89(bl),90,91,92,94(br),95, 99(bl),100,101,102,104(br),105,106,107,108,109.

Thanks to: Ella, Ellis, Eva, Jerzie, Nicolas, Shaan, Sophie & Thomas
Thanks to: Lorri Baker, Lee Dempsey, Scott Holden, Tracey Lushington & Jamie Watkins

Printed and bound in Spain by Edelvives

2018 2017 2016

11 10 9 8